WAR
TORN

Photographs by

Eddie Adams
Shlomo Arad
Coskun Aral
David Burnett
Richard Cross
Françoise Demulder
Arnaud de Wildenberg
Frank Fournier
John Hoagland
Peter Jordan
Cindy Karp
Alain Keler
Philippe Ledru
Harry Mattison
Don McCullin
Steve McCurry
Alain Mingam
Etienne Montes
Yan Morvan
Robin Moyer
James Nachtwey
Matthew Naythons
Roland Neveu
Michel Philippot
Bill Pierce
Olivier Rebbot
Eli Reed
Alon Reininger
Reza
Eugene Richards
Jean-Marie Simon

WAR TORN

Introduction by Thomas L. Friedman
Photographs Edited by Susan Vermazen
Designed by Roger Black

Sarah Lazin Books

Pantheon Books NEW YORK

Copyright ©1984 by Sarah Lazin Books and Susan Vermazen.
All rights reserved under International and Pan-American
Copyright Conventions. Published in the United States by
Pantheon Books, a division of Random House, Inc., New York, and
simultaneously in Canada by Random House of Canada Limited,
Toronto.

Library of Congress Cataloging in Publication Data
Main entry under title:

War torn.
   1. War victims—Pictorial works.   2. Military history,
Modern—20th century—Pictorial works.   I. Vermazen,
Susan.   II. Friedman, Thomas L.
D431.W36 1984   909.82'0880694   84-42703
ISBN 0-394-54061-1
ISBN 0-394-72684-7 (pbk.)

Manufactured in Italy

First Edition

In Memory of John Hoagland

Contents

Preface

EVERY WEEK we see hundreds of photographs from wars around the world. Newspapers and news magazines report the major events: battles, aerial bombardments, car-bombings. Combat shots are familiar, but there is another side to war that we rarely see—the ongoing story of people whose lives are irrevocably changed by forces over which they have no control. From my work as a photo editor and my contact with war photographers, I knew that these scenes had been recorded. More personal and more human than the images of war we know, these photos inspired *War Torn*. This book is an attempt to show ordinary people whose lives are shattered by conflicts they did not start and cannot affect. I found that my feelings were shared by many of the photographers. Whether or not they regarded a war as "justified" or thought one side was "right," they saw the tragic consequences.

I put together an initial slide presentation. After viewing this, many photographers dug out work that they had lost hope of ever seeing published. They talked to other photographers, who in turn sent in more photographs. The results are some of the most striking images in this book. To get their pictures, they use skill, timing, intuition, and caution. But sometimes that is not enough. Richard Cross and Olivier Rebbot were killed while on assignment in Central America. As this book was going to press, John Hoagland was shot dead in El Salvador.

War Torn is intended to be a record of the last ten years of work by these photographers and of the suffering of the people who live where wars are fought. This book is dedicated to all of them.

I would like to thank the many people at *New York* magazine, *Newsweek*, *Time*, *The New York Times*, and the International Center for Photography, too numerous to mention individually, who gave advice, suggestions, and time to this project.

I would especially like to thank James K. Colton, Robert Pledge, Peter J. Kellner, Robert Stevens, Hillary Raskin, Mark Bussell, and Fred Ritchen, who, whether or not they agreed with the final approach, have given invaluable advice.

I would like to thank Ed Kosner for his unfailing support and encouragement throughout the entire project.

For help in preparing the photographs and the text, I would like to thank Peter Blauner, Vivette Porges, Bonnie Steinbock, Don Alden, Stephanie Franklin, Janis Bultman, Peter Kaufman from Berkey K&L, Jonathan Maslow, Howard Chapnik, Ed Sturmer, Sarah Lazin, and Wendy Goldwyn.

SUSAN VERMAZEN

Introduction
By Thomas L. Friedman

One Plus One Plus One Plus One...

WHY do photographers and journalists go off to cover wars? I have often been asked that question and more often have asked it of myself and my colleagues. There are, I believe, two answers. The worst among us go off to wars because they provide the proverbial "bang bang" that gets on the front page, not to mention those rushes of excitement and close calls that are the stuff of countless dinner-party and barroom tales. Those same reasons, I suppose, motivate some people to become firemen, others commodity brokers. Never a dull moment.

The best journalists and photographers are attracted to covering wars for different reasons, reasons reflected in these photographs. Ultimately, they are seeking neither excitement nor scenes of grisly death, which can be found easily enough while covering local traffic accidents. They are there to learn more of life and people. What is most rewarding about covering a

Overview of Beirut, following the Israeli invasion (preceding pages). *Lebanon, 1982.*
YAN MORVAN

On her balcony in West Beirut, a Shiite Moslem woman (right). *Lebanon, 1982.*
STEVE McCURRY

war is discovering a whole new spectrum of human emotions and experiences that one would never witness outside this violent crucible. Places like Beirut and El Salvador are emotional frontiers, and it is along such frontiers that one discovers what human beings are really capable of doing, both good and evil. One observes people's unbounded compassion alongside their unfathomable insensitivity, their ingenuity alongside their astounding folly, and their madness alongside their infinite ability to endure. It's all there writ large.

The opportunity to chart these emotions and scenes, to capture them in a photograph or a lead sentence in a way that shows people something about themselves that they may never have realized before, inspires the best journalists and

Palestinian men and women in the Ain El Helwe refugee camp, which was destroyed during the Israeli invasion, search for food (preceding pages). *Lebanon, 1982.*
BILL PIERCE

Amid the rubble of his shop, which had been attacked by a rival Christian faction, a barber in Christian East Beirut (left). *Lebanon, 1982.*
STEVE McCURRY

Beirut—parts of which had been destroyed in 1976 —during the Israeli invasion of 1982 (below). *Lebanon, 1982.*
REZA

photographers to go to war. It presents an opportunity to learn and to teach at the same time.

What does one learn? That depends very much on the journalist or photographer and the situations he or she gets caught up in. But it is hard to cover a war without coming away with an acute appreciation for the sheer absurdity and randomness of it all. I remember once at the end of the Beirut siege of '82 a multistory apartment house packed with refugees was devastated in a mysterious explosion. At the time, people said the building had been hit by a "vacuum bomb," or some such science-fiction device, that had sucked all the air out of the building and caused it to collapse like a house of cards. But no one really knew; people just liked to talk. A woman who lived in the building hap-

Amid buildings in central Beirut destroyed in 1976, a street vendor sells his wares to workers and French troops (preceding pages). *Lebanon, 1982.*
ROLAND NEVEU

These three children of Tyre are going to church for the first time after a week of Israeli bombing (below). *Lebanon, 1982.*
YAN MORVAN

The Tyre hotel district during peacetime between two wars; rich Lebanese take a pleasure ride (right). *Lebanon, 1983.*
YAN MORVAN

pened to be standing outside when the place exploded; a nearby photographer captured her on film as she gazed in disbelief upon the smoldering mound that was once her home but was now a miserable tomb. The woman, tears streaming down her face, her mouth gaping open in shock, formed an unforgettable picture of grief and horror. Though held back by someone, she struggled to throw herself onto the rubble. To me this was one of the most powerful pictures of the war, because it illustrated so well what it really means to be an "innocent civilian" caught up in someone else's conflict.

But the story does not end there. Minutes after the picture was taken, a car bomb exploded just around the corner from the destroyed apartment building where the bereaved woman stood crying; it blew her apart in the midst of her grief.

An Independence Day parade in the Quiché Indian town of Nebaj features an army float. *Guatemala, 1982.*
JEAN-MARIE SIMON

Within a few minutes she was twice a victim—first a mourner, then mourned.

That scene always frightened me, maybe because it somehow drove home the point that no one is keeping score; that there is no referee up there saying, "Okay, this person has suffered enough. Bring on the next one." You could suffer terribly and still suffer some more. Or, you might not suffer at all. War chooses all its victims randomly.

News coverage, and particularly television, tends to focus almost entirely on one aspect of wars—the advances and retreats of armies, along with the killing and destruction they leave in their wake. What often gets lost in the drama of these great battle scenes is the fabric of life still clinging together. I was always struck by how often people would come to Beirut and say to me in amazement, "Why, I never expected

Soldiers march through Finca La Perla, an estate of three hundred people occupied by an army of seventy. *Guatemala, 1982.*
JEAN-MARIE SIMON

there to be so many buildings still standing," or "How do people live?" .

　　When a society is rent asunder by violence neighborhoods, individual apartment houses, and families tend to fall back on themselves and become self-sustaining cells that replace the larger unit. There are apartment houses in Beirut filled with strangers who organized themselves into co-ops during the Israeli invasion and other bouts of fighting. If someone came across fresh strawberries on the street, he bought not only for himself but for his neighbors as well. If someone had a generator, everyone crammed into his apartment at night to watch the news or to make an ice cube. (During the steaming summer of '82, when there was no electricity in West Beirut, a cube of ice was one of the nicest gifts anyone could give or receive.) People living through a war always seem to spend much

Teenage girls in a Salvadoran guerrilla school take a break from training (below). *El Salvador*, 1982.
CINDY KARP

Young Salvadoran girl from Usulután, where there had been a lot of fighting (right). *El Salvador*, 1982.
JAMES NACHTWEY

more time coping and adjusting than they do being afraid. People just don't have time to be afraid for very long.

The best way to cope, of course, is to maintain some kind of routine in one's life, and it is remarkable what risks people will accept in order to snatch a crumb of normality in the midst of some crisis. George Beaver, a ninety-year-old Beiruti, used to play golf almost every day during the Lebanese civil war. Plodding around the golf club of Lebanon by himself, Beaver would drive his ball past all sorts of wild-eyed gunmen, knowing that although he must be crazy to do this, he would be even crazier if he didn't.

It is this natural instinct to cope that makes for some of the most bizarre contrasts one encounters when living behind any battlefront. Two scenes come immediately to mind. The first took place in the Shatila refugee camp the day the September '82 massacre ended. An old woman came back to her house in the camp and found her entire family savagely butchered. The only thing left alive in her little cinderblock shanty hut was the family's yellow parakeet. The bird was chirping away in its cage, oblivious to the carnage it had witnessed. The woman walked out of her house wailing, gripping a framed picture of her murdered son in one hand and the caged, singing parakeet in the other.

The other scene took place three months earlier, on the morning of June 7, 1982—the day after the Israeli invasion began. I was sleeping in my Beirut apartment just after dawn when suddenly a series of earsplitting bangs echoed through the neighborhood. I jumped out of bed and crawled into the living room where I hoped to peek over the balcony to see what was firing. But as I slid along the floor toward the balcony window, all I could see was a calm aqua-blue Mediterranean Sea, framed between the lazy palm trees in the front garden. The gun was nowhere to be seen, only

Young Indian girl dances with an army soldier at an Independence Day dance in the Nebaj town hall in Quiché province, a former guerrilla stronghold. *Guatemala, 1982.*
JEAN-MARIE SIMON

After the coup against Allende, young adults—
many of them students—are rounded up
and held inside the National Stadium
(preceding pages). *Chile, 1973.*
DAVID BURNETT

These women were taken off a bus and
searched; later they were taken prisoner.
Rhodesia, 1979.
PETER JORDAN

Guerrillas force civilians out of their cars and buses
after blocking the Carretera de Litoral
highway. *El Salvador,* 1981.
ALAIN KELER

A Nicaraguan woman, having given these contras some food, is anxious about whether to accept money from them (pages 34 and 35). *Nicaragua, 1982.*
JAMES NACHTWEY

Somoza's army checks peasants before the Sandinista takeover (pages 36 and 37). *Nicaragua, 1978.*
OLIVIER REBBOT

Anti-shah demonstrators about to be executed in Teheran (below). *Iran, 1979.*
OLIVIER REBBOT

Soldiers frisk civilians in downtown Santiago during the roundup after the coup (right). *Chile, 1973.*
DAVID BURNETT

During the weeks before the Ayatollah Khomeni took power, police fire into a crowd that had gathered near a university (pages 40 and 41). *Iran, 1979.*
DAVID BURNETT

The army fires into a crowd of mourners at Archbishop Romero's funeral; seeking safety, many tried to crowd into the cathedral. Twenty to thirty people died in the chaos that ensued (pages 42 and 43). *El Salvador, 1980.*
ETIENNE MONTES

Lebanese man, with his wife and child, flees his house, which is being bombed (pages 44 and 45). *Lebanon, 1982.*
COSKUN ARAL

Man with dead child emerges from an apartment building that had been hit by a car bomb intended for the nearby French headquarters (pages 46 and 47). *Lebanon, 1983.*
YAN MORVAN

"People are the same the world over. Enemies, allies, they all have the common denominator of humanity. Not only are people the same, but the war is the same." DAVID BURNETT

A mourner at the funeral of Nobel Laureate Pablo Neruda, who had died ten days after the coup. This was the last open gathering of prominent people in the arts and people of the left. *Chile, 1973.*
DAVID BURNETT

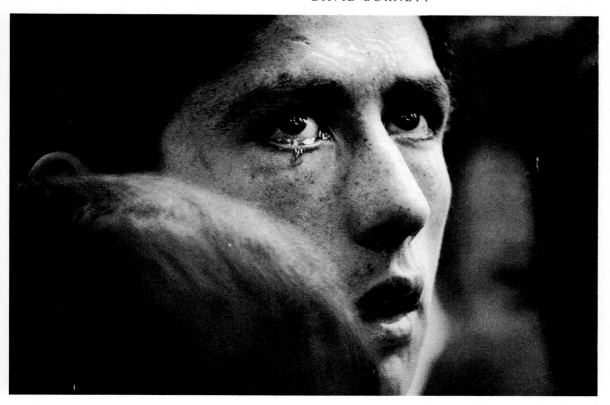

Palestinians try to escape the Christian Phalange
during the takeover of their camp at the
start of the civil war (preceding pages).
Lebanon, 1976.
FRANÇOISE DeMULDER

A Belfast man makes a futile attempt at putting
out the fire in a truck hijacked by the IRA.
Ireland, 1981.
JAMES NACHTWEY

A Belfast family passes a truck set afire by the
IRA. *Ireland, 1981.*
JAMES NACHTWEY

"My interest is in explaining to people what is going on in all these places, because you hardly ever get an accurate presentation, whether it's the newspapers or television. We live in one world, and with the communication so much improved, I think it's the media's duty to educate the public." ALON REININGER

During a lull in the fighting, two children walk by unexploded shells lying on a Tripoli street (preceding pages). *Lebanon, 1983.*
ELI REED

Following a small skirmish between the left and the military, residents use water to help sweep the blood into the gutter (right).
El Salvador, 1979.
ALON REININGER

Women check their houses and belongings after intense shelling at the predominantly civilian Baddawi Palestinian camp north of Tripoli (preceding pages). *Lebanon, 1983.*
FRANK FOURNIER

A León woman whose mother and two children were killed by a government rocket returns to the destroyed building in the now abandoned barrio, after the funerals (right). *Nicaragua, 1979.*
RICHARD CROSS

A Palestinian woman whose husband was murdered discovers the wreckage of her home (below). *Lebanon, 1982.*
DON McCULLIN

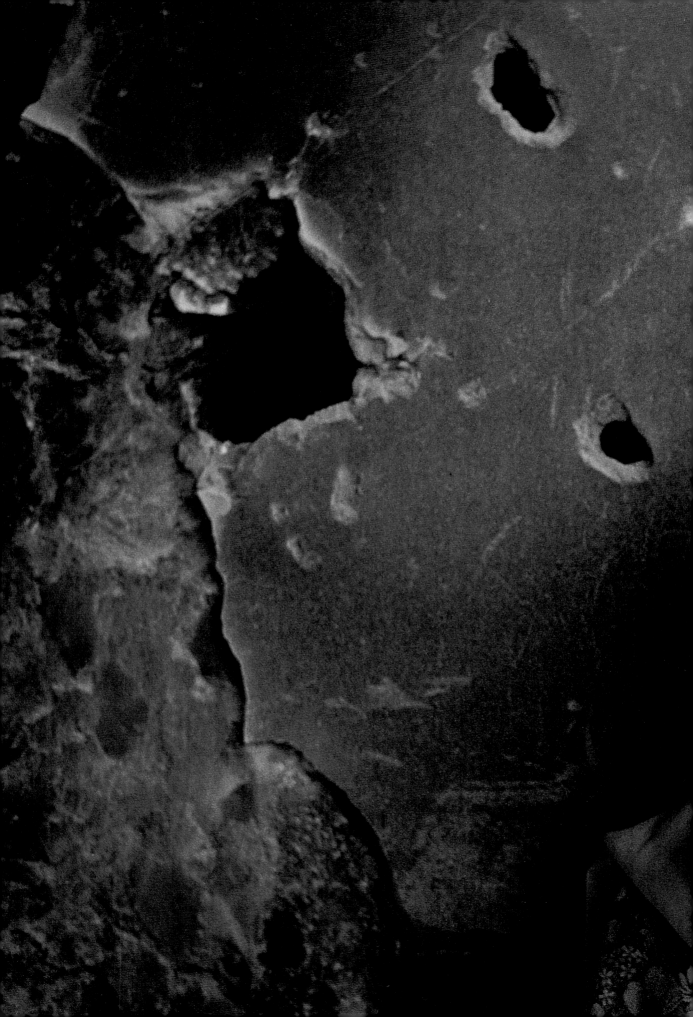

A Beirut woman stands against the wall of her shelled home, situated in the direct line of fire between Moslem militiamen and the U.S. Marines (preceding pages). *Lebanon, 1983.*
JAMES NACHTWEY

Kibbutz Misgav Am nursery, after an attack on Israel's northern border with Lebanon. The children had been held hostage and one was killed; it was the first day of Passover (right). *Israel, 1980.*
SHLOMO ARAD

View from the street: the remains of a Beirut house (below). *Lebanon, 1982.*
EUGENE RICHARDS

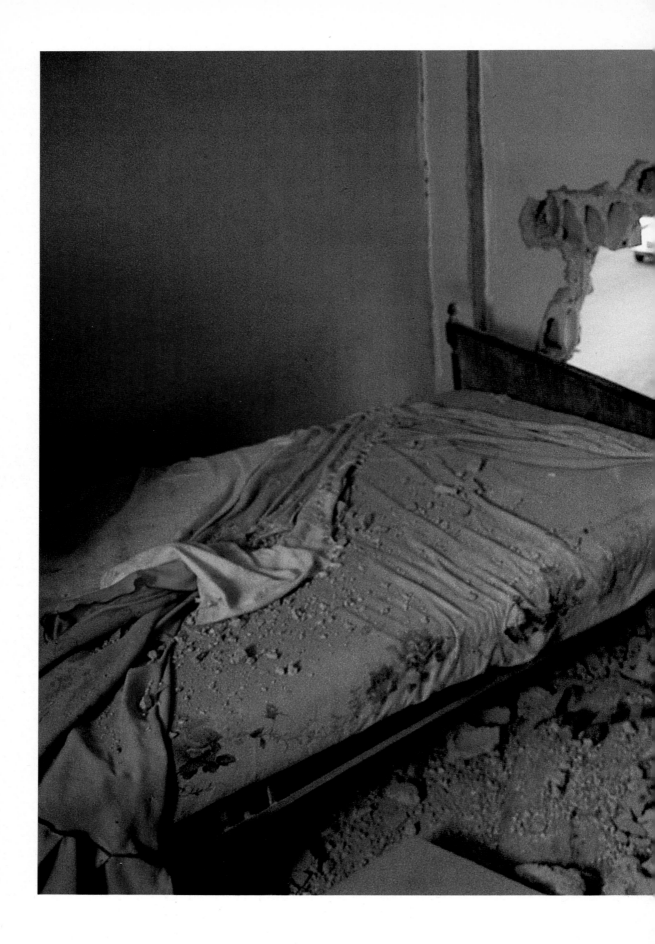

"There's nothing subtle about photographs. A broken wall and a living room. A couple of blown-out men in a blown-out building. There's not much in the way of truth or subtlety–there's just destruction."

EUGENE RICHARDS

A Palestinian woman from the Burj Al Barajneh camp seeks shelter from the shelling in the lower floor of a hospital in South Beirut (pages 66 and 67). *Lebanon, 1982.*
ARNAUD DE WILDENBERG

PLO camp Naher Bared resident stands in his house, where a shell had blasted the wall next to his bed (pages 68 and 69). *Lebanon, 1983.*
ELI REED

Patients in a mental hospital several weeks after it had been bombed (right). *Lebanon, 1982.*
EUGENE RICHARDS

Sudanese woman sits before her tent in an
Eritrean refugee camp (above). *Ethiopia, 1979.*
PETER JORDAN

The luxury Summerland Hotel in West Beirut, after
being shelled in the Israeli invasion (left).
Lebanon, 1982.
STEVE McCURRY

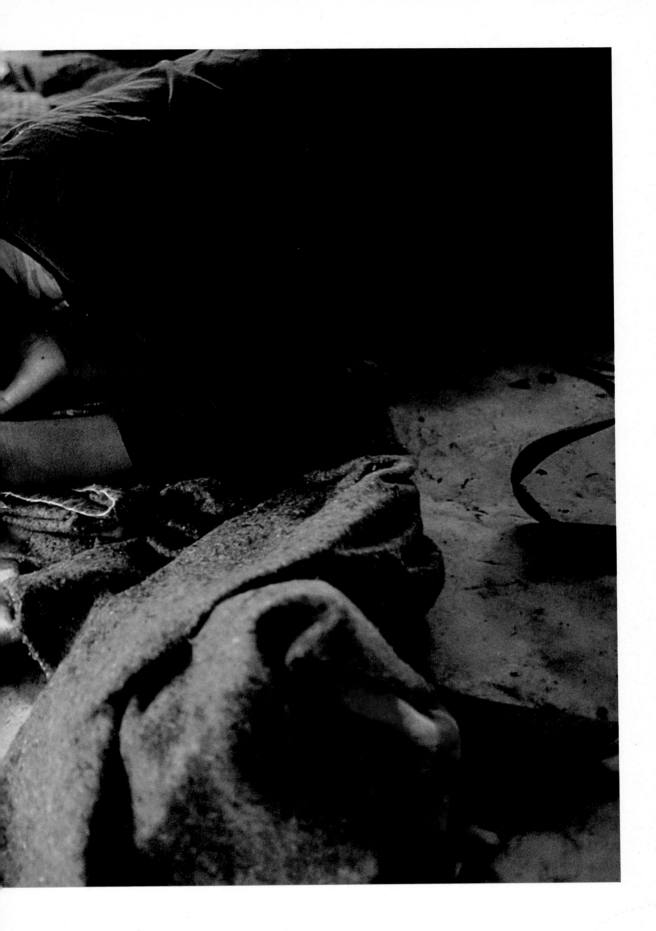

Nicaraguan refugee children in a makeshift camp across the border (above). *Honduras, 1983.*
JAMES NACHTWEY

A Cambodian refugee holding a baby in the nursery of a refugee camp (left). *Thailand, 1980.*
DAVID BURNETT

Cambodian refugee in Thailand, near the Cambodian border (pages 74 and 75). *Thailand, 1979.*
OLIVIER REBBOT

Refugees of Quiché province who have left their homes out of fear for their safety (pages 76 and 77). *Guatemala, 1982.*
ETIENNE MONTES

Afghani refugees whose village was bombed by the Russians set up tents on the outskirts of Peshawar, near the Afghanistan border (pages 78 and 79). *Pakistan, 1980.*
STEVE McCURRY

Salvadoran father and child in a refugee camp (page 80). *El Salvador, 1981.*
HARRY MATTISON

Cambodian refugee family struggling to reach the Thai border during the rainy season (page 81). *Cambodia, 1979.*
ROLAND NEVEU

A Lebanese child dives over a partially
submerged military truck. *Lebanon*, 1982.
MICHEL PHILIPPOT

Belfast Catholic children play near a burning barricade of trucks, set afire to keep out British soldiers. *Ireland, 1981.*
BILL PIERCE

"What I see is just this grotesque human obscenity, and all I try to do is say that this should not be allowed. Wars go right on in spite of my photographs, in spite of television, in spite of newspapers, in spite of magazines, in spite of still pictures, in spite of motion pictures. All the work that we do doesn't change a damn thing."   BILL PIERCE

A young boy, just out of the hospital after the siege of Beirut, greets a friend during a ceasefire (left). *Lebanon, 1982.*
YAN MORVAN

Shiite Moslem children play on a still-functioning Palestinian anti-aircraft gun near a refugee camp in South Beirut (above). *Lebanon, 1982.*
STEVE McCURRY

A young boy swings on a Somoza tank that the Sandinistas left behind as a monument to the revolution (pages 88 and 89). *Nicaragua, 1982.*
JAMES NACHTWEY

Cambodian children from the refugee camps along the Thai border run after a food truck (pages 90 and 91). *Cambodia, 1980.*
ROBIN MOYER

Khmer Serie boy in a refugee camp shows his drawing of life in Kampuchea under the Pol Pot regime (pages 92 and 93). *Thailand, 1979.*
ROBIN MOYER

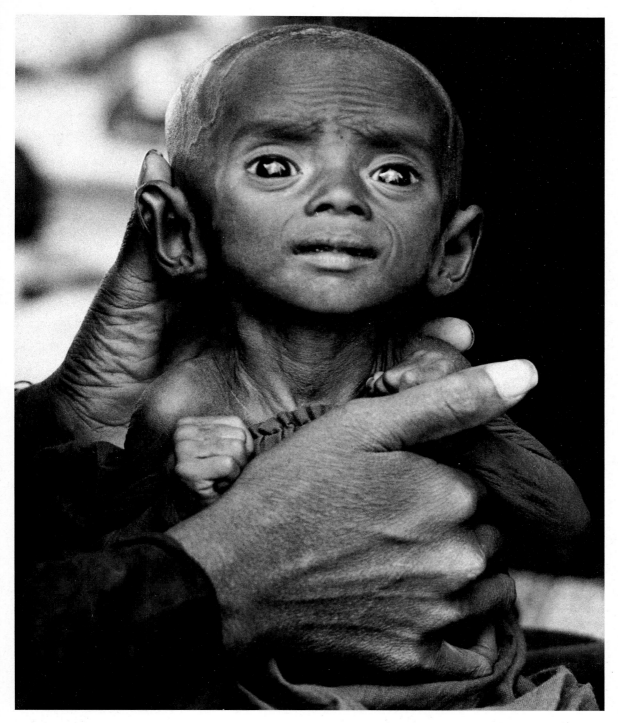

Cambodian children near the Thai border during the mass exodus (left). *Thailand, 1980.*
EDDIE ADAMS

A three-and-a-half-month-old baby in his mother's hands. The infant, who weighed only five pounds, was expected to die of malnutrition (above). *Thailand, 1980.*
EDDIE ADAMS

A young girl burned by an explosion of a phosphorus bomb lies in a Palestinian hospital in West Beirut. *Lebanon, 1982.*
ROLAND NEVEU

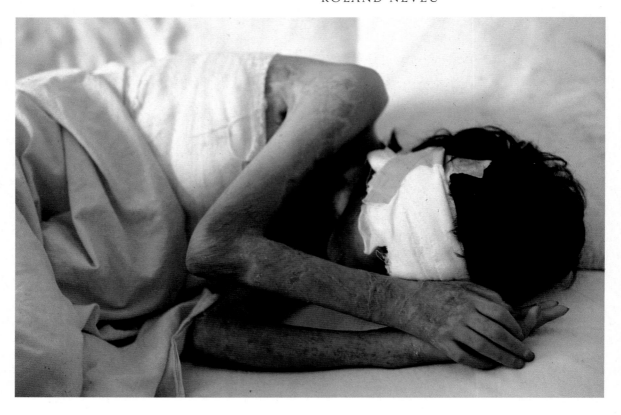

A man carries a dead child. Both are victims of Israeli bombing of South Lebanon (pages 98 and 99). *Lebanon, 1981.*
JAMES NACHTWEY

A victim of army aerial bombardment in Quiché, this young Indian refugee was rounded up with other Indians by the army. She is here at an army base on the way to relocation in a refugee camp. *Guatemala, 1983.*
JEAN-MARIE SIMON

A child in La Bermuda refugee camp dies in his father's arms. *El Salvador, 1981.*
HARRY MATTISON

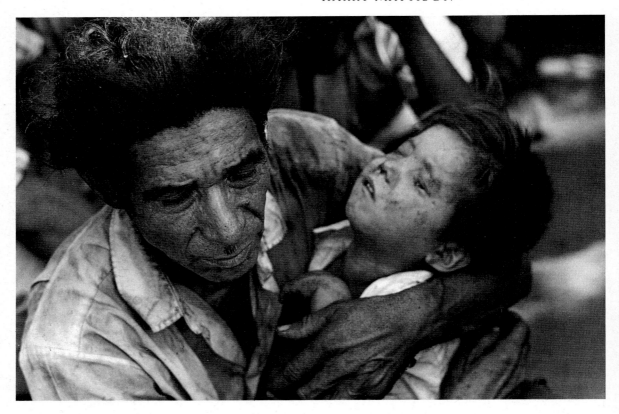

"One day a guy can be a hero and the next day he can be a villain. Salvador is not black and white. Lebanon is not black and white. These situations are one million shades of gray."

JOHN HOAGLAND

A woman holding her child discovers the body of her husband, a civil guard who was killed during fighting in Santa Clara. *El Salvador, 1982.*

JOHN HOAGLAND

A death squad victim floats in Lake Ilopango, near
San Salvador (preceding pages).
El Salvador, 1979.
ALAIN KELER

The Red Cross burns bodies of victims of a Somoza
air raid in León. *Nicaragua, 1978.*
MATTHEW NAYTHONS

Photographers document Maryknoll and U.S.
embassy staff exhuming the remains of
three American nuns and a lay missionary
who were murdered by Salvadoran troops.
El Salvador, 1980.
ALON REININGER

Demonstrators of the Ligas Populares, shot by soldiers (above). *El Salvador, 1979.*
ALAIN KELER

Relatives of victims of the Sabra-Shatila massacre (below). *Lebanon, 1982.*
ALAIN MINGAM

A soldier stands over a man killed by guerrillas in San Salvador (above). *El Salvador, 1981.*
OLIVIER REBBOT

The dead in the streets of Managua before the Sandinista takeover (below). *Nicaragua, 1978.*
OLIVIER REBBOT

The body of an old man, a victim of the shelling in a
Moslem section of Beirut. *Lebanon, 1982.*
PHILIPPE LEDRU

A school in Sidon where over a hundred children
were killed in a bombing; the bodies were
covered with lime. *Lebanon, 1982.*
BILL PIERCE

The "road of skulls": excavations of the mass
graves containing nearly 8,000 people
who were executed during the Khmer
Rouge rule (preceding pages). *Cambodia*, 1981.
ROLAND NEVEU

"This is us. What happens to them is what happens to us. And if something bad happens to them, then that evil or that unhappiness has happened to us also."

HARRY MATTISON

Anti-shah demonstrators dip their hands in lamb's blood symbolic of the "martyrs" killed by the shah's army. *Iran, 1979.*
OLIVIER REBBOT

Women mourning young Sandinistas who were killed on the northern border with Honduras while harvesting a coffee crop (left). *Nicaragua, 1982.*
JAMES NACHTWEY

Mourning a husband and young son, Protestants who were killed when their milk truck was attacked by rioters in a Catholic neighborhood (below). *Ireland, 1981.*
JAMES NACHTWEY

Palestinian mourners at the end of Ramadan in a
cemetery filled with the graves of soldiers.
Lebanon, 1982.
BILL PIERCE

Israeli woman at a Jerusalem cemetery on Memorial Day. *Israel, 1982.*
JAMES NACHTWEY

"You're outraged that people have to resort to this kind of behavior to settle their differences. And you feel that by communicating it, you're helping to make openings for understanding. To make an opening and say, 'Look, this is wrong. This is needless.'"

JAMES NACHTWEY

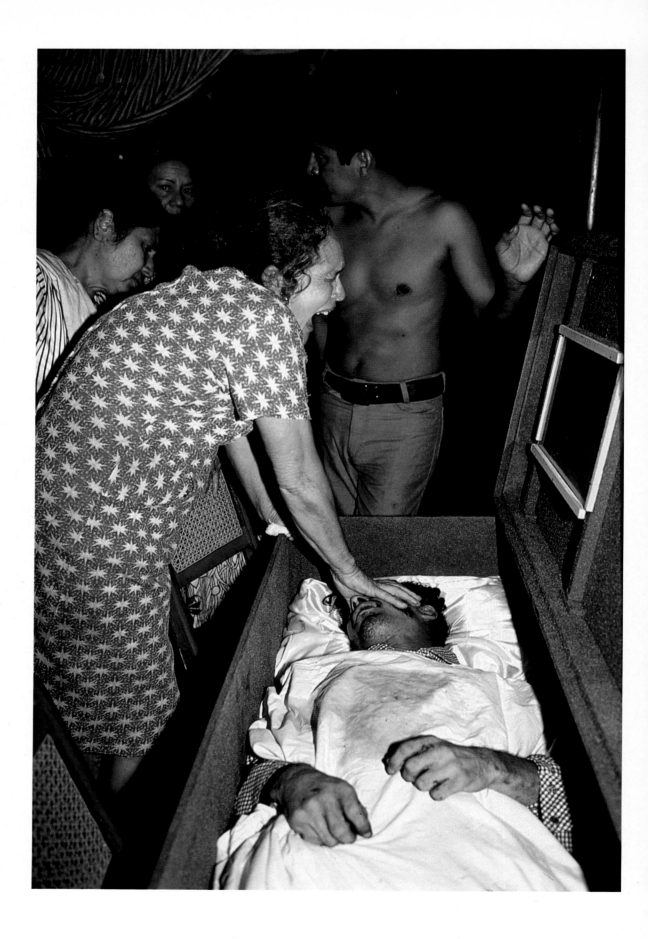

A woman touches her son, killed in crossfire
between Sandinistas and the military (left).
Nicaragua, 1979.
ALON REININGER

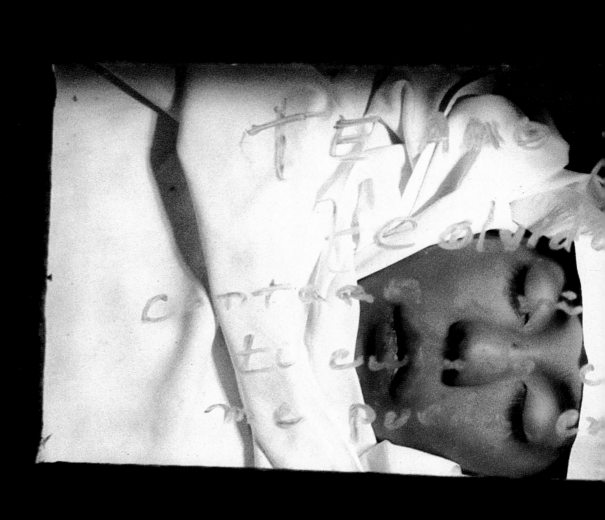

A widow mourns at the funeral of her husband, a Sandinista army officer killed near the Honduran border (pages 122 and 123). *Nicaragua, 1983.*
MATTHEW NAYTHONS

Woman killed in massacre of demonstrators in San Salvador. The writing on the coffin reads: "I love you. I will never forget you. I will tell my daughter about you when she grows up and can understand" (pages 124 and 125). *El Salvador, 1979.*
ALAIN KELER

About the Photographs

About the Photographs

The quoted material following the description of the photograph was taken from interviews with the photographer.

Pages 10–11, *Lebanon*, July 1982. YAN MORVAN—SIPA/Special Features.

Page 13, *Lebanon*, 1982. STEVE McCURRY.

"This is a Shiite Moslem woman living in West Beirut. The building in the background had been bombed by the Israelis some months before. I don't know how many people were killed, but she hadn't moved. They were already refugees from South Lebanon, so this was their last place. They were just staying there because they didn't have any place else to go."

Pages 14–15, *Lebanon*, fall 1982. BILL PIERCE—Sygma Photo News, Inc.

"This is a Palestinian refugee camp that was destroyed when the Israelis invaded Lebanon from the south. The camp had aerial bombardments, artillery, and then soldiers marching through it. Any military-age male not killed was taken prisoner. The rest were left to try to find food and stay alive."

Page 16, *Lebanon*, 1982. STEVE McCURRY.

"This barber was open for business. His shop had been hit several times before, so rather than repair the broken glass, he just proceeded with his business."

Page 17, *Lebanon*, June 5, 1982. REZA—SIPA/Special Features.

Pages 18–19, *Lebanon*, 1982. ROLAND NEVEU—Gamma-Liaison.

Page 20, *Lebanon*, July 1982. YAN MORVAN—SIPA/Special Features.

Page 21, *Lebanon*, July 1983. YAN MORVAN—SIPA/Special Features.

Page 22, *Guatemala*, September 15, 1982. JEAN-MARIE SIMON—Independent Visions International.

"The Independence Day parade in the Indian town of Nebaj included an army float on which some of the few non-Indian children in town were invited to ride. Nebaj, formerly a guerrilla stronghold, is now entirely controlled by the army."

Page 23, *Guatemala*, September 1982. JEAN-MARIE SIMON—Independent Visions International.

Page 24, *El Salvador*, February 1982. CINDY KARP—Black Star.

Page 25, *El Salvador*, 1982. JAMES NACHTWEY—Black Star.

"Even after days of fighting in the town of Usulután, the natural grace and innocence of this young Salvadoran girl seemed to balance the threat of continuing violence."

Page 27, *Guatemala*, September 15, 1982. JEAN-MARIE SIMON—Independent Visions International.

Pages 30–31, *Chile*, 1973. DAVID BURNETT—Contact Press Images.

"This was the day they took the press to the stadium to show that everyone was being well treated and well cared for. It happened to be the day after I'd been arrested outside the stadium; my cameras were taken from me and I was spread-eagled on the wall for half an hour. While I was in there, you could hear a lot of screaming. People were obviously being either beaten or tortured. The next day they took us in to see the place on a little media tour, and I asked if we could go downstairs. They said, 'Oh no, no. There is nothing going on down there.' But as they started to take us out, a bunch of soldiers appeared and right behind them the door opened, and half a dozen people came in with their hands over their heads. And as we were waiting there, I turned around and looked in the other direction and behind two other soldiers I saw a group of kids. This one guy looked at me with these eyes of steel."

Page 32, *Rhodesia*, 1979. PETER JORDAN—Gamma-Liaison.

Page 33, *El Salvador*, 1981. ALAIN KELER—Sygma Photo News, Inc.

"This was the second day of the big offensive of January 1981. Guerrillas stopped all trucks and cars going on this main highway and they turned them over and burned them so the highway would be completely blocked. They told the people that they should walk back. The funny thing about this picture is at first the people were scared in front of the guerrillas. They raised their hands. And then they walked for three or four kilometers and passed a small army post. It wasn't really a post, just some soldiers guarding the bridge. And the people passing in front of the soldiers just raised their hands the same way that they did when they passed in front of the guerrillas."

Pages 34–35, *Nicaragua,* 1982. JAMES NACHTWEY—Black Star.

Pages 36–37, *Nicaragua,* 1978. OLIVIER REBBOT—Contact Press Images.

Page 38, *Iran,* 1979. OLIVIER REBBOT—Contact Press Images.

Page 39, *Chile,* 1973. DAVID BURNETT—Contact Press Images.

"This was shot on a Sunday morning in Santiago when they were still arresting a lot of people. The army was trying to gather up all the extremists, leftists, anybody who had anything even in a remote way to do with the previous regime. A lot of people were more or less summarily shot . . . bodies were found all over town at night. This scene was in a middle-class neighborhood. I just started wandering around. The streets were relatively deserted. You would see jeeploads of soldiers going by now and then. I remember walking into the scene and seeing these soldiers bringing out boxloads of books and dumping them and burning them in the street. It was right out of *Fahrenheit 451.* I can remember just walking around and turning a corner and seeing this guy being put up against a wall. They frisked him. It was a very quiet thing. There was no pushing and shoving. I'm not even absolutely sure what happened to him. I suppose they probably took him away. But scenes like that were happening all the time."

Pages 40–41, *Iran,* 1979. DAVID BURNETT—Contact Press Images.

"This picture was taken after the shah left; the street demonstrations against the regime were building every day. The army was trying to display force all over town in ways that would bottle up the demonstrators and keep them under control. A lot of tear gas was going off and there was a lot of shooting. I was with some other photographers and we had heard a bit of shooting a while before and started walking that way. We got down to a corner near the university famous for a lot of action. All of a sudden shooting started and you could see people running in and out of the square. The tempo was interesting because there would be shooting and then everybody would run around and then would calm down, and people who would have taken cover would slowly start to wander back to where they could peek around the corner of a building half a block away and see what was going on. This picture was one of those moments where—in the middle of the calm—shooting started again. You just see all these different reactions to the shooting. There's heads turning. There's people immediately starting to run. There's people just standing there. And even though the picture is a little fuzzy, I think you still get a feeling of how all these different people each react in their own way to what is going on."

Pages 42–43, *El Salvador,* 1980. ETIENNE MONTES—J. B. Pictures.

Archbishop Oscar Arnulfo Romero was assassinated on March 24, 1980, as he said mass in a small chapel in San Salvador. Six days later 80,000 people gathered for his funeral.

"I was on the first floor of the Metropolitan Cathedral taking a general shot of the crowd. Suddenly I heard one explosion after another and saw a lot of smoke and confusion. The crowd panicked. The people were trying to get into the cathedral, but not all could get in. They tried to escape, but all streets were closed. They thought all corners of the square were surrounded by the Salvadoran Army and that the shooting was coming from the National Palace. Many of the wounded were pregnant women and old people who had been trampled by the crowd in the chaos. The panic lasted for half an hour, and after it cleared, the street was covered with shoes."

Pages 44–45, *Lebanon,* 1982. COSKUN ARAL—SIPA/Special Features.

Pages 46–47, *Lebanon,* October 23, 1983. YAN MORVAN—SIPA/Special Features.

Page 49, *Chile,* 1973. DAVID BURNETT—Contact Press Images.

"This picture was made during the funeral of Pablo Neruda, the Chilean poet who died about ten days after the coup. His funeral was the last for a long time. It was the last open gathering of a lot of people of the left, prominent people, and people of arts and letters. In its own way it was a protest against the coup. Because I think there were so many press people covering it, it became a miniature event, virtually unimpeded by the military. They sang the 'Internationale' at the cemetery. I remember one tall bearded man in the crowd. I don't remember what he said, but it was so eloquent people were in tears."

Pages 50–51, *Lebanon*, 1976. FRANÇOISE DEMULDER—Gamma-Liaison.

Page 52, *Ireland*, 1981. JAMES NACHTWEY—Black Star.

"Rioters continually burned hijacked vehicles in front of this man's small row house in West Belfast. One afternoon he had had enough and performed one of those magnificent gestures of futility for which the Irish have become famous."

Page 53, *Ireland*, 1981. JAMES NACHTWEY—Black Star.

"In a West Belfast neighborhood a young rioter hijacked and burned several trucks in honor of one of his friends who had just been released from prison. For those not directly involved in the repetitive acts of violence in Northern Ireland, life goes on, but not without a sense of distaste and resignation."

Pages 54–55, *Lebanon*, 1983. ELI REED—Magnum.

"This was in a PLO camp during the fighting between Arafat and Abu Musa. I had gotten into the camp that morning to try to take pictures and this is one of the things I saw—the big shell and people walking around it or running to wherever they were going. This kid had a package he had just bought, some food or something, and was on his way home to his family."

Page 57, *El Salvador*, October 1979. ALON REININGER—Contact Press Images.

"This picture was taken a little bit outside of the center of San Salvador, right after the military officers had pulled a coup against General Romero. The left came with a small force and they set a position on the street. The army came and there was a fight and some people got killed. I have no recollection—and I don't think they even asked—who died, whether he belonged to the left or was an innocent civilian. I suspect he was not from the neighborhood. They moved him with a whole pile of bodies to the meat wagon—one of those anonymous unmarked trucks that come after confrontations like that in the cities. They would just pack all the dead bodies in it; I gather these were the bodies that ended up in the canyon where all the vultures found nourishment."

Pages 58–59, *Lebanon*, 1983. FRANK FOURNIER—Contact Press Images.

Page 60, *Lebanon*, 1982. DON McCULLIN.

Page 61, *Nicaragua*, 1979. RICHARD CROSS.

Pages 62–63, *Lebanon*, 1983. JAMES NACHTWEY—Black Star.

Page 64, *Lebanon*, 1982. EUGENE RICHARDS—Magnum.

"I was just walking down the street, searching for what remained of normalcy. That's what everyone was trying to do, to correlate the Beirut that we'd heard about—the beautiful city—to what we saw when we were there, a broken-down and shell-shocked city."

Page 65, *Israel*, April 7, 1980. SHLOMO ARAD.

"The first day of Passover was the one time of year I join my wife's family for lunch. We had just walked in, the bleeper beeped: 'Arad move to Misgav fastest possible way.' That was the end of the annual family reunion. Misgav Am is a two-and-a-half-hour drive from Tel Aviv. Being that it was a holiday, the authorities were not quick to announce the PLO attack over the radio. When I arrived, the dead and wounded had already been removed. . . . I walked into the children's house where the kids were held hostage and what I saw was this sight as it appears."

Pages 66–67, *Lebanon*, 1982. ARNAUD DE WILDENBERG—Sygma Photo News, Inc.

"This old Palestinian woman came to the hospital during the day to try to get shelter. Too many people were in the hospital and there was no space for her. She went to the third-floor underground where shelling had exploded and damaged this car. The ray of light is coming from the ground floor, from a hole that was dug in the floor."

Pages 68–69, *Lebanon*, 1983. ELI REED—Magnum.

Page 71, *Lebanon*, 1982. EUGENE RICHARDS—Magnum.

"The two in the window were wandering around on the third floor of the mental hospital. I was on assignment and my job was to see if I could take some photographs of the Palestinians and how they were faring during the destruction of the city. I got out and walked around for a few days, kind of desperate because most of those people didn't care to be photographed. They thought we were Israelis and were keeping a record of them One of the places I ended up was the hospital, a week or two after it had been bombed. There hadn't been any repairs and a lot of nurses were afraid to come there because of the bombing. The walls had broken down, so there were flies everywhere. All the toilets were broken and the water was out. Most of the people were being kept down in the basement, away from the bombing. I went up a few floors in the building and there I saw these men who were just walking around."

Page 72, *Lebanon*, 1982. STEVE McCURRY.

"The Summerland had been a five-star luxury hotel built on the seafront in West Beirut. The Israelis claimed that it was a base for the Palestinians, so they bombed it very heavily. The place had been fifty percent destroyed, so it was amazing that the owner would rebuild a luxury hotel in Beirut, of all places. There probably hasn't been a tourist in Beirut in the last four years. The beach where the guests had stayed was still mined and an occasional fisherman would be killed right in front of the hotel."

Page 73, *Ethiopia,* 1979. PETER JORDAN—Gamma-Liaison.

Pages 74–75, *Thailand,* 1979. OLIVIER REBBOT—Contact Press Images.

Pages 76–77, *Guatemala,* 1982. ETIENNE MONTES—J. B. Pictures.

"These people who left their homes because of fighting had come to this area looking for safety. Sometimes army officers would come, and on this occasion a colonel came to give a speech about how bad the communists and the guerrillas are and how the army was there to protect them. The people, mostly Indians, were shouting, 'Down with communism' and 'Long life to the government.' "

Pages 78–79, *Pakistan,* 1980. STEVE McCURRY.

Page 80, *El Salvador,* 1981. HARRY MATTISON.

Page 81, *Cambodia,* October 1979. ROLAND NEVEU—Gamma-Liaison.

Page 82, *Thailand,* 1980. DAVID BURNETT—Contact Press Images.

"We walked into the camps, and I started wandering around and ended up in the nursery. I'm sure that's the hardest it's ever been in my whole life to take pictures. These little kids, from newborns to seven, eight, ten years old . . . starving was part of it, but it wasn't just that. Their faces had so much pain and trauma and horror in them; it angered me to see that. There were faces that five-year-old kids were not supposed to have. Children are not supposed to react like that. God knows what they've been through, what they've seen. It made me feel like a real intruder just being there with a camera, but I wanted to photograph it and I wanted people to see it and feel the same outrage that I felt."

Page 83, *Honduras,* 1983. JAMES NACHTWEY—Black Star.

"Nicaraguans who fled their country for a makeshift refugee camp in Honduras found squalor and hopelessness. They could neither return to their own country nor enter into the life of a new one. At first they were not even recognized by relief agencies as refugees and were therefore ineligible for aid."

Page 84, *Lebanon,* September 1982. MICHEL PHILIPPOT—Sygma Photo News, Inc.

Page 85, *Ireland,* 1981. BILL PIERCE—Sygma Photo News, Inc.

Page 86, *Lebanon,* 1982. YAN MORVAN—SIPA/Special Features.

Page 87, *Lebanon,* October 1982. STEVE McCURRY—Copyright © 1983 National Geographic Society.

"When I took this picture, the war had been over for a couple of months. There was a lot of live ammunition still lying around over the city, but particularly around these anti-aircraft batteries. So the kids were just swinging and playing, rotating the barrel. The gun still functioned. I don't think they would have shot it, but the kids could still move the turrets. There were grenades and rockets and land mines all over the city but particularly in this area."

Pages 88–89, *Nicaragua,* 1982. JAMES NACHTWEY—Black Star.

Pages 90–91, *Cambodia,* 1980. ROBIN MOYER—Black Star.

Pages 92–93, *Thailand,* 1979. ROBIN MOYER—Black Star.

"In October of 1979 a major Vietnamese offensive and the effects of the prolonged war in Kampuchea forced tens of thousands of refugees into the border area near Aranyaprathet in Thailand. A combination of starvation, malaria, and dysentery was exacerbated by the overcrowded camps.

"This young Khmer Serie boy in Khao I Dang refugee camp spent his day drawing pictures of what life was like in Kampuchea under the Pol Pot regime. He did not speak."

Page 94, *Thailand,* 1980. EDDIE ADAMS—Gamma-Liaison.

Page 95, *Thailand,* 1980. EDDIE ADAMS—Gamma-Liaison.

Page 96, *Lebanon,* August 1982. ROLAND NEVEU—Gamma-Liaison.

Page 97, *Guatemala,* April 1983. JEAN-MARIE SIMON—Independent Visions International.

Pages 98–99, *Lebanon,* 1981. JAMES NACHTWEY—Black Star.

"In the summer of '81, Israeli jets bombed and burned South Lebanon, which was being used by the civilian population as well as the PLO military. When the plane struck, this bridge was being heavily used by civilians and many died. This man must have known that the child was dead."

Pages 100–101, *El Salvador,* 1981. HARRY MATTISON.

"This refugee camp was filled with over a thousand people. The army had come in and they were taking out people whom they suspected of being guerrilla collaborators, and were executing them. I saw one man with a child who was extremely sick, and I went over and started talking to him. I took the first photograph and then I put my camera down again, and then the child started coughing. And then the child died. It all happened very quickly."

Page 103, *El Salvador*, 1982. JOHN HOAGLAND—Gamma-Liaison.

"I got into town about twenty or thirty minutes before the fighting was over. Usually in these types of situations everybody barricades themselves in their houses. This woman's husband had been out on a defensive mission that night and he'd been killed in fighting and she came out of the house. There were about three or four of them in this one position and they'd all been killed. Their families came out and found them."

Pages 104–105, *El Salvador*, 1979. ALAIN KELER—Sygma Photo News, Inc.

Page 106, *Nicaragua*, 1978. MATTHEW NAYTHONS—Gamma-Liaison.

"I photographed this in 1978 after a Somoza air raid on León. *Figaro* ran it in 1982 and said these were bodies of Miskito Indians and then Haig said this is proof of Sandinista atrocities against the Miskitos. The Red Cross was going around yelling, 'Hay heridos y muertos,' in a real singsong voice, almost like a melancholy chant. They found the bodies and as part of the Central American wartime ritual they burned rather than buried them."

Page 107, *El Salvador*, 1980. ALON REININGER—Contact Press Images.

"It was several days after the nuns were killed, and the exact location and the death information seemed to have gotten to some clergy in Washington. It got back to the American embassy and the Maryknoll order in El Salvador, and they went to locate the grave. They started digging, and as they got to the first limb, it became very clear that they'd found the right grave."

Page 108 (top), *El Salvador*, October 29, 1979. ALAIN KELER—Sygma Photo News, Inc.

"A leftist group called LP-28, the Ligas Populares, were having a small demonstration in downtown San Salvador. The preceding night a bomb had exploded at one of the two main newspapers, so some soldiers were guarding the paper. Apparently they panicked when they saw the demonstrators and they started shooting. The shootout lasted for quite a while."

Page 108 (bottom), *Lebanon*, 1982. ALAIN MINGAM—Gamma-Liaison.

Page 109 (top), *El Salvador*, 1981. OLIVIER REBBOT—Contact Press Images.

Page 109 (bottom), *Nicaragua*, 1978. OLIVIER REBBOT—Contact Press Images.

Page 110, *Lebanon*, June 1982. PHILIPPE LEDRU—Sygma Photo News, Inc.

Page 111, *Lebanon*, 1982. BILL PIERCE—Sygma Photo News, Inc.

"These are the remains of a young child from the school in Sidon that was hit by a bomb. Over one hundred children were killed; the school was destroyed. The children were outside the basement of the school, on the outskirts of the building. This child couldn't make it to the shelter, although even children in the shelter were killed. There was no way to bury the children, so they spread lime over the bodies."

Pages 112–113, *Cambodia*, January 1981. ROLAND NEVEU—Gamma-Liaison.

Page 115, *Iran*, 1979. OLIVIER REBBOT—Contact Press Images.

Page 116, *Nicaragua*, 1983. JAMES NACHTWEY—Black Star.

"Members of the Sandinista youth volunteered to go to the northern frontier of Nicaragua to help harvest a coffee crop. They were attacked by anti-Sandinista guerrillas and seventeen of them were killed. The mass funeral was held in Managua the day before the Pope arrived."

Page 117, *Ireland*, 1981. JAMES NACHTWEY—Black Star.

"This Protestant woman lost her husband and fourteen-year-old son in the same incident. They had been delivering milk in a Catholic neighborhood when their truck was attacked by rioters reacting to the hunger strike by Irish Republican prisoners. They had been delivering milk to the same area for years, but when the political climate changed, they were suddenly perceived as enemies."

Page 118, *Lebanon*, 1982. BILL PIERCE—Sygma Photo News, Inc.

Page 119, *Israel*, 1982. JAMES NACHTWEY—Black Star.

Page 120, *Nicaragua*, June 1979. ALON REININGER—Contact Press Images.

"This picture is from Chinandega. There was a confrontation in the barrio between the left—the Sandinistas and the sympathizers of the Sandinistas in the neighborhood—and the military, the soldiers of Somoza. This guy didn't belong to any of the groups. He just happened to be there."

Pages 122–123, *Nicaragua*, Easter Sunday, 1983. MATTHEW NAYTHONS—Gamma-Liaison.

Pages 124–125, *El Salvador*, 1979. ALAIN KELER—Sygma Photo News, Inc.

"This is one of the dead of a demonstration of the LP-28. A few of the people had camped in one of the churches in San Salvador, and nobody would move in and chase them away. So they had these dead bodies lying on the floor for a couple of days and one day I went into this church. Suddenly I saw a woman moving toward the coffin and she started writing something on the glass window. After she wrote, I took the picture."

About the Photographers

About the Photographers

Eddie Adams

SIX YEARS AFTER he joined the Associated Press, Eddie Adams won a 1969 Pulitzer Prize for his coverage of the Vietnam War. Since 1972, Adams has been under contract to *Time* and *Parade* magazines. He has covered events in Jordan, Egypt, Turkey, Cyprus, Portugal, Lebanon, and Ireland. Among the more than five hundred awards Adams has won are the George Polk Award (1969, 1977, 1978), the Sigma Delta Chi award for news photography (1969, 1977, 1979), the National Press Photographers Association/University of Missouri Pictures of the Year's Magazine Photographer of the Year award (1975), and the Overseas Press Club of America's Robert Capa Gold Medal (1977).

■ ■ ■

"People have different interpretations of what a good photograph is. My interpretation is that a photograph could have absolutely no composition, could be totally out of focus, could have everything wrong in terms of art in photography, but if you as a viewer look at that picture and it did something for you, it's a good picture."

Shlomo Arad

BORN IN AUSTRIA in 1937, Shlomo Arad moved to Israel after World War II with the Youth Immigration Program. Arad's assignments have taken him to the Mideast, Cyprus, Yugoslavia, Austria, Germany, and Italy; he has been working for *Newsweek* since 1977. He is the recipient of the Anna Rivkin Bruk Prize (1973) from Sweden. His photographs have been collected in *Bedouin, the Sinai Nomads* (1984), and other books.

■ ■ ■

"I was born in the 'war zone' and have been searching all my life for the 'peace zone.' Having been both a refugee of war and a combat soldier, photographing a war is more than a professional experience for me. The first war I covered only as a photographer was the October War in 1973, but living in Israel is really living war, or the danger of it, all the time.

"In the wars I have covered so far, I always joined a fighting unit and headed for the front line with them. I simply cannot do it any other way, both professionally and emotionally. I have to remain with the story until it's over.

"I think that being with a fighting force, you get to feel both the 'good guys' and the 'bad guys.' You certainly come to learn and feel that there are no heroes in a war. Everyone is a victim."

Coskun Aral

SINCE 1977 Coskun Aral has been photographing events in his homeland, Turkey, as well as in Iran, Iraq, Poland, Ireland, Afghanistan, and Lebanon. In 1980 he was awarded the Grand Prize for Journalism in Turkey.

David Burnett

AT AGE TWENTY-ONE David Burnett began working at *Time* magazine, where he later became a contract photographer. He later worked for *Life* magazine and traveled to the Mideast, the Far East, and South America. Burnett was awarded the Overseas Press Club of America's Robert Capa Gold Medal (1973). His other awards include the Overseas Press Club's Best Photographic Reporting from Aboard (1979) and the National Press Photographers Association/University of Missouri School of Journalism Pictures of the Year's award for Best Magazine News Photograph (1980).

• • •

"I think the reason you're there is to tell the story, to tell what's going on. If you're going to be a Red Cross worker, go be a Red Cross worker, but don't be a photographer. If you want to be a negotiator for Amnesty International, do that. Don't be a photographer. That doesn't mean you can't care about it. You should care about it. But your primary function is to communicate to other people who aren't going to be there, who don't know about it, what's going on."

Richard Cross

AFTER TWO YEARS of working at the Worthington, Minnesota *Globe*, Richard Cross joined the Peace Corps. He was stationed in Colombia where he became interested in the Palenqués; his photographs appeared in the book *ManGombe: Warriors and Herdsmen of Palenqué* (1979). Cross was killed on June 21, 1983, along with a reporter when their vehicle was destroyed by a land mine in Honduras.

Françoise Demulder

SINCE THE MID-SEVENTIES, Paris-born Françoise Demulder has covered events in Southeast Asia, Cambodia, Laos, the Mideast, and Angola. For the last six years, she has been working in the Middle East and is currently based in Beirut, where she works for *Time* magazine. She was awarded the World Press Photo Prize (1977).

Arnaud de Wildenberg

BORN NEAR PARIS in 1954, Arnaud de Wildenberg began photographing conflicts around the world in 1979, first in Afghanistan, then in Iran, Southeast Asia, Lebanon, Uganda, Somalia, Israel, Jordan, Poland, and elsewhere. He was named the Best News Reporter of the year by the Paris *Match* (1980). His work has appeared in several books, including the cover of *A Day in the Life of Australia*.

Frank Fournier

WHEN HE WAS THIRTY years old, Frank Fournier decided to become a photographer. Since then his work has taken him to Bolivia, Surinam, Nicaragua, Honduras, France, Germany, Lebanon, Spain, Morocco, and elsewhere for *Time* magazine and other publications.

John Hoagland

IN 1977 John Hoagland became a stringer for the Associated Press and United Press International in Central America. In 1980 he began covering El Salvador for *Newsweek*. In 1981 he was put under contract to the magazine and he moved to El Salvador, where he continued to cover events there as well as in other areas including, in 1984, Beirut. On March 16, 1984, Hoagland was killed on assignment when caught in crossfire between the Salvadoran army and the guerrillas.

• • •

"I find it's hard because when you're shooting, it doesn't affect you—the camera is a shield. And even though you see everything through the viewfinder, you're putting something between you and what's happening.

"I have a lot of problems with the word *objectivity* because it's really a Western idea. Everybody has their opinions, and even when you try to be objective, you're going to have them. I find that I won't be a propagandist for anybody, on any side. You do something right, I'm going to take your picture. If you do something wrong, I'm going to take your picture also.

"I was so much braver in my first war. In some ways ignorance is bliss. The first time you really don't know how scared you should be. The second and third war, when you really understand what it's about . . . I'm not as brave as I used to be. You try to play your odds—you always think you can get away with it. I take the part that there are two things in life. One, I know if I do it long enough, the odds are going to catch up with me. I understand that fully. Secondly, I ain't going to get away with it. You have to go on your instincts. Some days you do everything wrong and nothing happens to you. There's no real rationale to it."

Peter Jordan

BORN IN LONDON in 1946, Peter Jordan began his photojournalism career in the early seventies in Rhodesia where he worked at a local newspaper. For the past six years his work has appeared in *Time* magazine, and he is the recipient of the Overseas Press Club's Olivier Rebbot Memorial Award for Best Photoreporting from Abroad (1983).

Cindy Karp

CURRENTLY BASED IN Mexico City, Cindy Karp works in Mexico and Central America. She has also been a staff photographer for United Press International and now is under contract to *Time*.

Alain Keler

BORN IN FRANCE, Alain Keler has photographed in India, Southeast Asia, Portugal, Italy, Iran, Cyprus, Poland, El Salvador, Turkey, Yugoslavia, Guatemala, Lebanon, and Israel. As a member of New York's SoHo Photo Gallery, Keler organized an exhibit of his photographs taken in India and Southeast Asia.

Philippe Ledru

AFTER STUDYING architecture, Philippe Ledru decided to become a professional photojournalist. Assignments have taken Ledru to Iran, Lebanon, Poland, the Soviet Union, Africa, Asia, and Central America.

Harry Mattison

PHOTOJOURNALIST Harry Mattison has covered events in Central and Latin America, Europe, and the Middle East. A contract photographer for *Time* magazine, Mattison also coedited (with Susan Meiselas) *El Salvador—Work of 30 Photographers* and has received the Overseas Press Club of America's Robert Capa Gold Medal (1983) for his work in El Salvador.

■　■　■

"You want to be as aware as you possibly can, but everything inside of you wants to shut down, push away all of this violence. And that contradiction is very difficult. It is even more difficult for those who are living their daily lives, who are used to being conscious and sensitive, and then are thrown into situations over which they have no control.

"You go into a situation of maximum violence. That violence can be psychic and/or physical, and you want to be as open as you possibly can, if you're going to be aware and sensitive. But the two seem to be contradictory.

"Watching somebody die is different than the evidence of a spiritless body. Watching somebody die has another effect. Fear. Fear of one's own mortality. Sadness and grief for the absence of a human's being. Pity. Rage. Rage that people should be allowed to die, and more specifically children, who have had so little of their lives already.

"If you want to know about the politics, you have to know about the culture you want to understand. And you have to have a basic respect for these situations and you have to have a respect for the people that you're dealing with. And the way that you acquire that respect is through knowledge.

There's a code of objectivity for many people in journalism—which is a lie. It's impossible to be objective. Personally, I prefer a passionate subjectivity.

"Photographers are no more important than any other professionals. These are practitioners. And the photograph is an artifact. But neither the practitioner nor the artifact is as important as the reality. And what we're talking about is reality. It's not about stories. Stories are something that are made for magazines. What's really important is reality."

Don McCullin

SINCE 1964, Don McCullin has covered events in Cyprus, the Congo, Rhodesia, Vietnam, Cambodia, Biafra, India, Bangladesh, Israel, El Salvador, and South America. He is the author of *The Destruction Business*, *Heart of Darkness*, *The Palestinians* (with Jonathan Dimbleby), *Homecoming*, and *Beirut, a City in Crisis*. He is the recipient of the Warsaw Gold Medal.

Steve McCurry

IN 1975 Steve McCurry became a staff photographer on Philadelphia's *Today's Post* and two years later became a freelancer. He has covered events in India, Nepal, Thailand, Pakistan, Bangladesh, China, Afghanistan, and Lebanon. His coverage of the Afghan war won him the Overseas Press Club's Robert Capa Gold Medal Award in 1980, and in 1982 a group show, "Afghanistan Today," exhibited his pictures. He won the Toronto Art Directors Club Gold Medal Award in 1983 for Editorial Photojournalism.

Alain Mingam

FRENCH-BORN photojournalist Alain Mingam has covered events in Portugal, Angola, Greece, Afghanistan, Lebanon, Iran, and the Middle East. He is currently vice chief editor in charge of the news for Gamma-Liaison. In 1981 he was awarded the World Press' third prize. Mingam has exhibited his work from Afghanistan in France.

Etienne Montes

IN 1975 Etienne Montes' first major assignment took him to the Sahara Desert. He has covered events in Africa, Spain, and Central America, including Nicaragua and El Salvador (where he lived for a year), and Belfast.